21 STEPS TO BECOME AN AWESOME PUBLIC SPEAKER

YOUR 3-WEEK POCKETBOOK OF INSPIRATION TO PRESENT LIKE A PRO

Jordana Borensztajn

LONGUEVILLE
MEDIA

A catalogue record for this book is available from the National Library of Australia

First published 2019 for Jordana Borensztajn by

Longueville Media Pty Ltd
PO Box 205 Haberfield NSW 2045 Australia
www.longmedia.com.au
info@longmedia.com.au
Tel. 0410 519 685

The information provided in the book is presented solely for educational and entertainment purposes on the subjects discussed. It is the intent of the author to provide information of a general nature. The author is not a registered psychologist or professional counsellor, financial planner, adviser, accountant, medical practitioner or legal advisor. The information in this book is not intended to be taken as (or be in substitution for obtaining) independent professional medical, legal, tax, business, financial, marketing or any other type of advice. In the event that you use, misuse or rely on any of the information in this book, the author assumes no responsibility or liability for your actions and its consequences including without limitation, any loss, claim, damages, costs or expenses. The author makes no warranties or representations about the accuracy of the information or the suitability of the information for your personal circumstances.

Front and back cover design: Bryan Webb (www.bryanwebbmedia.ca). Under exclusive licence in perpetuity to Jordana Borensztajn for this book and other related works.

Front cover art element, image credit: iStock.com/urfinguss

ISBN: 978-0-6485107-0-3

Dedication

For everyone who dreams
of becoming a public speaker,
it's time to turn fear into fun!

CONTENTS

INTRODUCTION

Powerful presentation skills are so important, yet most of us are afraid of public speaking. It tops almost every fear list ever compiled, which I find crazy!

We live in a world filled with funnel-web spiders, black mamba snakes, tiger sharks, and processed ham in a can. That's *truly* scary stuff. Yet most of us find it *way* more petrifying to stand on stage, behind a podium, in an air-conditioned ballroom. Huh? How does that make any sense? What are we so afraid of?

The number one reason is the fear of judgement and criticism. We're scared of stumbling over our words and looking like an idiot. We *convince* ourselves that this will damage our reputation and that we will never, ever, ever, ever recover from the humiliation, no matter how long we live.

This fear can feel so overwhelming that it totally paralyses us. Well, in this book I'm calling BS on that because public speaking is an art form which, like every other creative discipline, can be learnt, practised, and mastered. So, let's work together to knock public speaking off the fear list and get arachnophobia back to number one, where it belongs.

Who's with me?

Yayyyyy.

When you're just starting out, public speaking can feel terrifying. This bite-size pocketbook is designed to help you kick-start your journey to confident public speaking with 21 easy steps that you can use to grow and develop your public speaking toolkit. It's short and fun, and is designed to make you laugh while you learn. You can read one step a day for 21 days, or 21 steps in one day, in any order you want – whatever works best for you.

Whether you're speaking at a conference, selling a product, pitching an idea, or just trying to convince your partner to actually listen to you for once, you can apply these steps to any situation to help you deliver your message in a clear and concise way that captures attention.

But enough about you – let's talk about me!

Every stage of my colourful career has involved creativity, courage, writing, rewriting, pitching, presenting, and continuously overcoming my fears.

From photography to journalism, from newspapers to radio, from print to digital, and from performing in comedy clubs to delivering keynote presentations and workshops in the corporate world, I've learnt the hard way about what works and what doesn't – with lots of highs, lows, and sleepless nights in between. I've made plenty of mistakes and learnt so many incredible lessons.

This mini-book is a culmination of the best insights and tricks I've picked up along the way. It contains some of the most powerful lessons I wish somebody had taught me at the start of my speaking journey. So, to save you years of trial and error, I've written this book to fast-track your progress, so you can speak with less pain and more LOLs!

In my public speaking workshops and coaching sessions, I have the privilege of witnessing transformation in front of my eyes. My students grow, evolve, and transcend their perceived limitations to passionately and powerfully express themselves. Their incredible growth excites me, motivates me, and inspires me to continue doing the work that I love – which is helping you.

So if you're reading this pocketbook right now, thank you. Whether you purchased it in a bookstore, bought it on Amazon, or "borrowed" it from your colleague's desk, all roads lead to the same place... and right now, you're here with me and I'm honoured. By picking up this book, you're making an important commitment to grow, develop, and step outside of your comfort zone.

If public speaking is on your bucket list, wish list, or even top fears list, this pocketbook – literally designed to slip into your back pocket before you get up on stage – will provide you with doses of inspiration to help you connect with your audience, conquer your stage fright, and replace fear with fun, so you have the courage to communicate with confidence when sharing your unique ideas, stories, lessons, and insights with the world.

Let's begin!

THE GIANT ELEPHANT
IN THIS TINY BOOK

Before we jump into the steps, I want to first address the elephant in the room: **creative fear**.

Fear is the greatest obstacle to our creative growth. And it's the scariest part of every new endeavour and project we embark on… especially public speaking.

Anything that involves putting our work and ourselves 'out there' – whether it's delivering a speech, creating a piece of art, or writing a new book – comes with a level of fear. *Will people like my book*? *Will they learn from it*? *Or will they use it as a coffee cup coaster*? Don't answer that!

It's easy to come up with dozens of reasons why we shouldn't embark on creative projects, and it's easy to listen to those voices of doubt, of scepticism (See Step 7: Turn off your inner critic). While fear can take hold at any time, it generally reaches its peak the moment we decide to share our work with the world… aka Judgement Day. And wow, is it terrifying!

Now, I'm no stranger to fear. Aside from being an arachnophobe (spiders), a melissophobe (bees), and a non-caffeinophobe (I made that last one up, but it's still horrifying), I've faced fear through every stage of my career. And it never, ever feels good. Fear feels like a dark, dense wall of nerves that stands between us and our new dream. And while this wall can feel impenetrable, we can always break through it to find the light.

Endless experiences of coming face to face with my own fears have taught me that nerves are temporary... but the regret of not taking a creative risk that lights up our soul can last much longer. Do you know how many people have wished they could have shared or pursued a creative idea or passion but were too afraid? Now, I don't know the exact number, but I imagine it's millions… zillions, even. So, don't be one of the zillions – we have enough of them already.

Be the person who pushes through your creative fears. Because once you've broken your fear barrier once, it's easier to do it a second time, and then a third. We each have the ability to change our threshold of fear.

And the most incredible part is that you never know what doors will open, and who you'll inspire when you find the courage to step into your light.

Smile. It's contagious.

We have a 7-second window to make a positive first impression. That's nothing! That's from now, 2, 3, 4, 5, 6, until now.

So, when you hit the stage, shine your pearly whites. Smiling is the universal symbol for happiness, and it has so many benefits. When you're smiling, you radiate joy and warmth, and it adds to your stage power and presence.

I know this sounds simple, but so many speakers have **serious face**. You don't have to stand on stage looking like The Joker but show your audience that you're genuinely enjoying yourself up there. If you hit the stage smiling, your audience reflects that back to you and you'll carry that positive energy through your whole presentation.

Here are a few fun facts about smiling:
- It's more contagious than a cold.
- It's easier to smile than it is to frown. *Seriously. Try it.*
- Smiling increases our body's natural happy drugs and makes us feel good.
- And – major bonus – smiling makes us way more attractive!

When we smile, it instantly makes us feel better. Say the following sentence without smiling: *'Thanks for having me. I'm so happy to be here today.'* OK, how did that feel? Pretty average?

Now, put a giant and genuine smile on your face and repeat the same sentence: *'Thanks for having me. I'm so happy to be here today.'* How do you feel? More alive? And how do you look? Sexier than a minute before? *Yeah, I'll bet you do.*

You can feel a massive difference when you're smiling, and your audience feels it too. So, use your beautiful smile to spread happy chemicals through the room when you're presenting.

STEP 2

Breathe through your nerves

If you're feeling stage fright, *do not* picture your audience in their underwear. Trust me, it never works. On many levels.

When we get nervous before a presentation – whether we're presenting to three people, our colleagues, or a room full of strangers – our physiology can take over. When our mind perceives a threat, our body prepares for danger, which is commonly known as the 'fight, flight, freeze' response.

Our body is going: *What do we do, guys? Do we run, attack, or stand still?* Most presenters either freeze or *maybe* run off stage if they're really scared. I've never actually heard of a public speaker attacking the audience out of fear. *Can you imagine?*

It's really common to feel butterflies in our stomach, to feel a tight chest, to get cold hands, sweaty palms, knocky knees, and tense muscles. These are normal physiological responses which, in the caveman era, served us well. Now, however, when we get scared or stressed, our body goes through exactly the same responses, but we're not being chased by wild animals – unless you're presenting with Sir David Attenborough, in which case, carry on...

When our physiology takes over, it can feel like we're out of control. The best way to manage your stage nerves is through your breathing. If you can control your breath, you can control your body.

A fantastic technique I learnt through Feldenkrais, an exercise therapy and body movement approach, is to take a slow and deep breath in for 4 seconds, hold it for 2 seconds, and then let it out for 4 seconds.

Breathing has so many benefits. It calms you down, it gives you a central point of focus, and as a bonus, also keeps your organs functioning and your body alive. Plus, calm breathing helps distract you from worrisome thoughts like *OMG the audience can totally see my sweat marks!* Try using the 4–2–4 model or create your own breathing rhythm.

STEP 3

Don't aim for perfect

Often when we're presenting, we want to do the best job possible. We want to be **perfect**. Any perfectionists out there reading this right now? *Hi…*

We can get so preoccupied with aiming for perfect that it adds pressure, and heightens our anxiety and our nerves, which ends up working against us.

Well, I have a ground-breaking secret for you, dear readers. Are you ready?

Perfect doesn't exist.

Seriously.

The truth is, perfect is the enemy of success. Why? Because, firstly, perfect is subjective. What you love, what I love, and what your boss loves might be completely different. And, secondly, when we present on stage, there are so many factors that are simply out of our control. If we aim for perfect we're holding ourselves up to impossible standards, because there is no benchmark for 'perfect'.

So, forget the old saying *Practise makes perfect,* and instead go with *Practise makes better*! Because *that* is actually true. Plus, your audience wants connection, engagement, honesty, and free food… not perfection.

So, don't aim for perfect. It doesn't exist.

STEP 4

Expect to be nervous

If you care about your presentation and you're passionate about your topic, you're going to feel nervous.

It's actually a good thing. It means you care.

Ask any public speaker, musician, or performing artist that you know and everyone – if they're being honest – will admit to feeling nervous. It's all part of the game. Nervous energy is a plus because it pushes us to do the best job we possibly can.

My advice is don't resist it. It's when we go: *OMG, I wish I wasn't nervous, I wish I wasn't panicking, I wish I didn't feel like I could throw up right now* that we create extra anxiety. When we push against our nerves, they get 10 times worse, because we're creating more resistance.

If you understand what's happening in your body when you're feeling nervous, you can manage it. So say to yourself: *OK, cool, I understand my physiology is getting ready for performance mode. My hands feel clammy, my heart's beating fast, I have butterflies in my stomach. What am I going to do? I'm going to do my breathing exercise. Breathe in for 4 seconds, hold for 2 seconds, breathe out for 4 seconds* (See Step 2: Breathe through your nerves).

Challenge the fear you feel. Whether it's one hour before, eight hours before, or a whole week before, your nerves will kick in before you present. Acknowledge that nervous energy simply comes with the territory of public speaking and stay one step ahead.

Know your audience

Every audience needs something different because every audience is unique. Your job as a speaker is to know who you're speaking to. So, find out as much as possible about your audience before you present.

Who are they? What's important to them? What challenges do they face? What's their blood type? OK, well, maybe not that last one. *Too much information.*

Understanding who they are is crucial. It influences how you structure your presentation, the stories you use, your language, how you dress – everything! It helps ensure you craft a presentation that will actually resonate. After all, you need to know *who you're speaking to* in order to know *how to speak to them.*

Because the truth is – *drum roll* – your presentation isn't about you! It's about your audience. I know this can be hard to hear because I know you've spent hours scripting, researching, and picking the right shoes, and now – all of a sudden – I'm breaking the harsh news that you're not number one. They are. *(What?!)*

The truth is, your role as a speaker is to transfer a message: to teach, to educate, to provide insight, to inspire, to make your audience laugh. And if they don't laugh, to bribe them with chocolate.

No? Just me? OK…

It's so easy to get immersed in ourselves when we present. We can get so focused on our content and wrapped up in our nerves that we focus on ourselves instead of focusing on our audience.

Remember: Your time on stage isn't about you. (Yay for public speaking!) It's about what you give to your audience. It's about the message, the lessons, and the insights you share. It's about what your audience can take away from your presentation and apply to their own life to create change – that's what it's all about. That's the magic of being an awesome public speaker.

STEP 6

Outline your presentation goals – for you and your audience

Whether you're an ad-libber by nature or your style is *I-must-write-out-every-word-of-this-script-right-now*, it's crucial you outline the goals for your presentation before you get up on stage.

So many times we can deliver a great presentation but we get off stage and realise we didn't *actually* cover any of our key points. (Panic mode!) Why did we do this? Because we went off on a tangent.

The best way to avoid tangents is to identify your presentation goals *before* you begin. Do you want to educate? Do you want to entertain? Do you want to inspire? Why are you getting up to present? And how will you ensure you reach your goals?

So many presentations can miss the mark because speakers haven't crafted and designed their intended outcome.

Our goals impact everything: Our opening, our storytelling, our speech length, the props we use (yes, it's OK to use props... we all need a little more colour in our lives). You *must* know what you want to achieve to ensure you *actually hit it* on stage.

Likewise, you also need to outline the goals for your audience. Because, as I've said before, your presentation isn't about you (See Step 5: Know your audience).

Your presentation is about what you *give* to your audience. So, always identify what you want them to take away from your talk. Is it to learn? To laugh? To feel motivated? What lasting impact do you want your presentation to have when your speech is over?

Remember: Clear goals create the best outcomes.

STEP 7

Turn off your inner critic

Sometimes our biggest creative enemy is…
ourselves. That's right! You and me. When we
launch a new project, a creative idea, or we
put ourselves out there with public speaking,
we all have an inner critic that can feed into
our fears and doubts, and in the worst-case
scenario, exaggerate *our* worst-case scenario.
Double trouble!

Our inner voice can be cruel. It can encourage
us to drop the microphone and tear up our
speech, saying things like: *You can't do this, you
loser! Get out! Nobody wants to hear a speech
from someone who is having such a terrible hair
day, anyway.*

Ouch.

Or our inner critic can show up right after we
present, with harsh blows like: *You spoke too*

quickly! You spoke too slowly! You missed a point! You should have worn a different dress!

Do you guys know that voice? Always remember your inner critic is a total jerk and should never be listened to. I know this can be challenging, because our inner critic knows our weaknesses and can find an endless number of points to pick on.

Before you present, while you present, and after you present, remember that your goal is to help others. So, don't focus on what you 'could, would, or should' have done differently. There's a difference between learning from your mistakes (See Step 18: Embrace your mistakes) and being self-critical. One is helpful and one is potentially damaging.

So, don't give your inner voice any power over you, unless it's giving you fabulous compliments. Drown out any negativity by paying attention to the positives. Focus on rewarding your epic efforts and celebrating what worked well, and then do more of that next time you present!

STEP 8

Add humour to your presentation

Humour is a really powerful tool for speakers because it allows you to create an instant connection with your audience. No matter who we are or where we're from, we all love to laugh.

And, amazing news, we can all learn to be funny. Yes, you read that correctly... Like many other creative and writing disciplines, comedy is an art form. There are rules and formulas in comedy theory that can be taught and put into practice by everyone.

Sure, we can't all riff like Joan Rivers and Jerry Seinfeld, but there are equations being used by the best in the business that you can apply to add a little more sparkle to your speechwriting.

One easy formula is the simple 'rule of three'. In literature, a list of three carries a special charm:

Three little pigs
Lights, camera, action!
Ready, set, go!

A list of three presents a brilliant opportunity for a joke because of the pattern set by items one and two. When you replace item three with something unexpected – *a turn* – that surprise makes us laugh.

For example: Top 3 tips for small business owners:

1. Prepare a plan
2. Prepare your finances
3. Prepare to not sleep... at all

Or, a favourite of mine: 'I'm not fussy about my dates. I just want them to be kind, thoughtful, and featured on the BRW Rich List.' *(I'm not asking for much, right, ladies?)*

Even a small dose of humour can have huge benefits. When you make your audience laugh, they like you more *and* are more likely to remember your messages.

Important warning: Do not write, create, or share humour that is offensive, divisive, racist, sexist, political, misogynistic, shameful, or hurtful. Aside from that, you have plenty to work with! (See Step 5: Know your audience)

STEP 9

Make eye contact

In this age of digital distraction, eye contact has never been more important. So, look into your audience's eyes (cue Bryan Adams).

Don't just scan the room, look down at the floor, stare at your notes, or randomly look up at the chandeliers… because if you do, your audience will feel disconnected from you.

Instead, intentionally look at different members of the crowd. It shows you're engaged and present and, importantly, makes your audience feel like you're in a *conversation with them*, rather than *speaking at them*.

A crowd is often the scariest aspect for a presenter, because there are living, breathing humans with all eyes looking at you – *and only you*. But in reality, your audience is one of the best parts of your presentation because they're like a live thermostat. You can instantly gauge whether you're hot… or whether you're not. In other words, how well your speech, content, and delivery is resonating and being received.

You can literally see how well you're engaging your audience by watching them.

So, take the time to look from audience member to audience member. Eye contact helps you create personal connections *and* genuine connections. The more you connect with your crowd, the calmer you'll feel, because you'll know you're communicating your messages effectively.

As they say, our eyes are the window to our soul.

STEP 10

Don't be scared of your audience

As I've said previously, I am not going to be the person who tells you to picture your audience naked. *Bad idea* (See Step 2: Breathe through your nerves). But I do want to urge you to *not be afraid* of your audience. Remember, they're on your side.

Your audience wants you to succeed as much as you do. You're all on the same team. Very few people give up their valuable time or purchase tickets to watch a speaker, or attend a conference, thinking, 'Ugh, this speaker is going to be horrendous. I can't wait to waste an hour of my life watching this train wreck!'

What happens to us as speakers when fear takes over is that our mind immediately jumps into an *Us vs. Them* mentality and we can feel like it's *Speaker vs. Audience*, which is wrong. Our inner critic goes: *They're judging me, they're critiquing me, they'd all rather be at cocktail hour right now!*

All this does is heighten our stage fright and anxiety. So, silence your inner voice by remembering… It's *your* voice and not your audience's.

Your audience is actually excited to hear a good presentation. They're supporting you by investing their time. Why? Because they're hoping to gain something, to feel inspired, and to find a lesson in your story that they can apply to their life to create change.

Remember: Your audience wants your presentation to be awesome, even if your fear tells you otherwise.

Cut the fat (from your script)

It's very easy to ramble and waffle on when we're presenting. Why? There are two main reasons.

One: When we are in front of an audience, we either get really nervous or super excited, both of which can wind us up and propel us straight into blabber mode.

Two: Often we just pack far too much content into our script.

If you've written a presentation, speech, or notes, and you have it nearby, please grab it now.

I don't want you to panic, but cut out everything that is not essential to your message, otherwise known as *fluff*. Go on, be ruthless with your editing. C'mon, I'm waiting… I know it hurts, but trust me, you're doing the right thing.

OK, have you done that? Is your blood pressure OK? Excellent. Now, wait 24 hours and edit it

28

again. I know it sounds like cruel advice, and editing out your precious words can be painful, but the truth is, we all believe that everything we have to say is *the most important thing in the world*. I know this first-hand. The first draft of this tiny pocketbook was the size of an encyclopaedia. That wouldn't look good in anybody's pocket!

Every speech can be cut, edited, trimmed, and delivered in a tighter and punchier way, which is better for you, and more importantly, better for your audience. The more you sharpen your message before you get on stage, the clearer it will be. Plus, there is always a greater chance that your time on stage will be cut down rather than extended.

So, edit and edit, and cut and cut, until you reach a point where you say, 'I can't believe I thought I needed those extra 120,000 words!' You'll feel so much lighter, and so will your audience.

STEP 12

Bring your personality to life on stage

Your audience develops a relationship with you the moment you step on stage. So, don't try to be like everybody else. Your most powerful asset is your uniqueness and your individuality.

When you're presenting, be yourself. Bring your personality to life on stage and use it to connect with your audience.

Everything you've lived through and learnt up until this point has converged to give you a brilliant, one-of-a-kind view that you're here to share. I believe that, in both business and in life, our differences are our greatest creative strengths. So, highlight your passions, your skills, your strengths, your expertise, and your point of difference, because that's what your audience connects with.

Sometimes, stage nerves can take over and we go into robotic presentation mode, where we lose our flow, our animation, and our personality, hiding behind a podium or a well-crafted slide deck. Try your hardest not to lose yourself when you're presenting. Be the you *on stage* that you are *off stage*, just… accentuated.

We connect with speakers on an emotional level, and the best speakers capture our hearts, minds, and imaginations. They share a true part of themselves with their audience. So, don't be afraid to show people how you're different and why your message is worth listening to, and worth remembering. Expressing your individuality and your uniqueness makes you stand out.

True passion is contagious, and the truth is, we do the best work when we love what we're doing. The more passionate you are on stage, the more enthusiastic you'll be, and the more your audience will connect with you *and* your message.

STEP 13

Have fun on stage

We're attracted to good energy. So, if you're having fun while you're presenting, your audience will have fun watching you.

There are actually more benefits to having fun on stage than you might initially think.

First up, even if your topic is serious, *you* don't have to be. Having fun can help you bring light to dark issues and communicate them in an engaging and meaningful way.

Second, if you can go with the flow and enjoy your time on stage, things that are out of your control won't bother you. When you're on stage, mobile phones go off, glasses and plates smash, some people start doing yoga stretches in their chair… we see really weird stuff from the stage! If you're open and fluid, these distractions won't faze you.

If you're on stage and nerves kick in, your body and face can stiffen up, and that stiffness radiates out to your audience, creating a disconnect. This means that instead of being immersed in a speaker's content, an audience can easily be distracted by the panic they're observing. They'll be thinking, 'OMG, she's so nervous! Her mouth is really dry. Can't somebody get her some water? Has she stopped breathing?' They can get so distracted, they'll tune out and won't even hear what a speaker is saying.

So, a great way to keep the energy high and the panic low is to have fun on stage. If you carry a fun energy, your audience will engage with your positivity, which means you will develop a better connection and they'll be more open to listening to – and hearing – the ideas and messages you're sharing.

If you're really fun, your audience members might even stay off their mobile phones. *Gasp!*

STEP 14

Practise as much as possible

The best way to plan and prepare for public speaking is... to plan and prepare! Don't just wing it.

There are generally two types of speakers:

1. The planners: They prepare and write out every single word of their script.
2. The ad-libbers: Perhaps they'll prepare some bullet points, but generally they'll present 'off the cuff'. Whatever comes out in the moment just comes out.

No matter where you sit on the scale, and where your individual strengths lie, practising your presentation is crucial. When you're presenting, there's an expectation that you're an expert in your topic, which means you *need to know* your content inside out. Even if you like improvising and being spontaneous, fight your instincts and plan ahead. Winging it does not look professional.

If you're a mad script writer, practising gives you freedom, because it means your eyes won't be glued to your script. If you're an ad-libber, practising helps ensure you're not the guy who rambles on and on without actually addressing the three key points in his speech titled 'The 3 Key Points for Success'.

Most of us experience presentation nerves, including butterflies, sweaty palms, shortness of breath, and knocky knees (See Step 4: Expect to be nervous). If you're winging it, and you get nervous on top of that, it will make your job way harder. So, make life easier for yourself! It sounds too simple, right? Well, I can assure you that a little bit of practise goes a long, long, *long* way...

Practise in the mirror, for a friend, for your Uber driver, or on the toilet – whenever and wherever you can. Become as familiar as possible with your content. Then, when you hit the stage, your presentation will be polished and cohesive. Plus, if you're confident in your content, you'll have more fun on stage because your focus won't be on remembering your speech. Instead, you'll have more freedom and energy to be playful and engage with your audience.

STEP 15

Inflect your voice

We all have amazing physical tools to help bring our messages to life on stage, but often we just forget to use them. One extraordinary tool is the incredible range and power of our voice.

Inflecting our voice is a simple technique that wields a huge impact. Inflecting involves changing our pitch, tone, or volume to give emphasis to certain words for expression and added meaning.

If we whisper, people lean in to hear our message, because whispering implies intrigue and mystery.

If we speak loudly, we add depth and power to our message, which helps us command the stage.

If we emphasise certain words, it keeps the audience engaged and also keeps us from sounding monotonous… Yippee!

So, think of your voice as a tool you can manoeuvre to enhance the message that you're delivering and the journey you're taking your audience on.

When you're preparing your speech, take out a highlighter and mark words, sentences, or phrases to emphasise, or to change in tone, pitch, and volume, to deliver them differently.

The more of our senses we engage, the more engaged we are. So, use inflection to take your audience on an auditory journey. Vocal variety makes your presentation way more exciting for you to deliver, and way more exciting for your audience to listen to.

STEP 16

Insert pauses… They. Are. Powerful.

Pauses are crucial, and a powerful tool for presenters. In comedy we call a pause a *beat*. And, as you know, timing is everything when it comes to delivering an awesome joke.

Often when we're presenting we don't pause enough because we're nervous, jittery, and just want to get through our talk as quickly as possible. Or, we're trying to cram too much content into a short presentation and end up feeling rushed.

But pauses are *so important*. They add emotion… and drama… and emphasis to our message. Pauses help you pace yourself. They give you control over your content and help anchor you to ensure you don't catapult into ramble mode.

Speaking fast with no breaks can be really overwhelming for your audience.

A pause gives the crowd a chance to digest what you're saying.

Just a heads up that, when you're presenting, a pause will feel wayyyyyyyy longer to you, as the speaker, than it will to your audience. But don't worry, because the truth is you're just giving your crowd time to... *phew*... time to breathe.

So, pause... for effect.

STEP 17

Use your hands to express yourself

A common issue that presenters face is: What do we do with our hands when we're presenting?

When we feel nervous, it's natural to start fidgeting. We'll shuffle our notes, wriggle our watch band, and twist the microphone cord so hard that we cut off blood circulation to our fingertips. *Not a good look.*

Your audience picks up on all these small details. You would know – as an audience member yourself – you can spot nervous movements a mile away.

So, here are a few things to avoid:

- Don't put your hands behind your back – it creates distance between you and your crowd.
- Don't put your hands in your pockets – it can make you look awkward.

- Don't cross your arms – it creates a barrier between you and your audience.

In everyday conversation, we naturally use our hands to express ourselves, so we should be using them on stage too. Your presentation is an open and fluid discussion between you and your audience. Even though you're doing most of the talking, your audience is listening and you're communicating back and forth in every moment, with every single word, and every single gesture and movement.

So, intentionally use gestures to emphasise your messages. Look through your script and find words, phrases, and sentences that lend themselves to expression and animation, and practise different ways to bring them to life.

Remember, there's only one of you on stage and possibly hundreds of people in your crowd. That means you're always going to look much smaller on stage than in real life. Using hand and arm movements helps you create a greater impact.

STEP 18

Embrace your mistakes

We're all human and we all make mistakes. *Especially in public speaking.*

Every time we present, there are *always* things we wish we had done differently, or we wish we had done better. We need to embrace our mistakes and be encouraged by the lessons they teach us, instead of dwelling on them with shame and regret.

I'm not saying making mistakes feels good. In fact, I would liken the feeling of making a mistake in front of an audience during the early stages of your speaking career to the feeling of someone tearing your insides out. It can be rough, I get it!

But don't give yourself a hard time. Instead, bring in a playful spirit (See Step 13: Have fun on stage) and be open to experimenting with your unique public speaking style.

The mistakes we make on stage are important. It's in our mistakes that we find key insights and lessons that are integral to our growth.

So, after you present, write down what you wish you could have done differently. Literally get it out of your worried mind and onto paper. And keep a list to ensure you're always making improvements.

A word of caution: This isn't a call to be hypercritical – no, no, no. Instead, it's an opportunity to use every experience you have in front of a live audience to positively inform and influence your future presentations. It's a strategy to self-improve.

Because, as we all know, a mistake is only a mistake if we don't learn from it.

So, *get ready to make mistakes* and *don't be scared of them*. You'll soon realise they're nowhere near as terrifying as you think they are. In fact, learning to manoeuvre around mistakes on stage actually becomes really fun. (And let's be honest, our mistakes make for some of the best dinner party stories!)

STEP 19

Inspire yourself with positive self-talk

Before you get on stage, it's really important to say the right things to yourself. The language we use – including the way we speak to ourselves and about ourselves – has a massive impact on our confidence levels and the faith we have in our own performance ability.

If you're about to get on stage, and you have negative thoughts running through your mind, like: *I'm going to stuff up; The audience won't like me; I'm not going to do a good job; I wish I was on the couch eating chips…* then your mind is feeding your body with negative messages and you're making it way more likely that you will in fact experience a negative outcome.

But don't panic. There's an easy way to resolve this: Replace any negative thoughts with positive self-talk.

Say to yourself, *This is going to be fun!* or *I'm excited to share my ideas with the audience,* or *I know my content inside and out – I've got this!* Our mind feeds our body and our body feeds our mind[1], so take the reins and trigger your mind-body process with positivity. And do it with a smile (See Step 1: Smile. It's contagious).

Positive messages in your mind send positive messages to your body, lifting both your energy and enthusiasm. You're in charge!

---

1 Dr Joe Dispenza, *Breaking the Habit of Being Yourself: How to Lose Your Mind and Create a New One*, Hay House Inc., Sydney, 2012, p. 57.

STEP 20

Dress to impress

Given that we live in a society where, unfortunately, a lot of people judge a book by its cover, what you choose to wear on stage is important. Your audience will size you up in a flash – wardrobe choice included.

Now, I don't claim to be a fashion expert, so I won't tell you what to wear, but I will say that when presenting, it's always safer to dress up than to dress down. Nobody is ever going to say, 'Can you believe he wore that great-looking suit and tie on stage? Horrifying!'

It's not going to happen. You can rarely look too formal… but it's very easy to look underdressed.

Even if you want to connect with your audience in a really cool and casual way, it doesn't mean you need to wear tracksuit pants and flip flops.

Bad move. It shows disrespect for your crowd when you haven't put in the effort to look presentable – *as a presenter*.

To bring out 'the best you' on stage, you need to feel confident. And what we wear, and how we present ourselves, has a huge impact on our confidence levels. So, choose an outfit that enhances your confidence; an outfit that makes you look and feel awesome.

Side bar: If you're filming your presentation, also consider an outfit that is timeless. You don't want to be that speaker who, a year later, sends out clips of their keynote presentation wearing a fluorescent tube top that came back into fashion for a brief 48 hours.

Choose an outfit you'll be happy to watch yourself in today, tomorrow, and in many more YouTube views to come.

STEP 21

View your time on stage as an opportunity

Here's a secret, and possibly my favourite step of all...

If you shift your focus from you as the presenter to the value you can bring to your audience, it changes absolutely everything!

I used to get so worried: *What if I don't remember my content? What if I run over time? What if the audience doesn't like me?* It was all about me, me, me. Which was wrong!

Now I say to myself: *My goal is to do the best job I possibly can, and to bring as much joy as possible to my audiences. I want to entertain, educate, and inspire others.*

That's the mindset to go in with. I focus on positivity and adding value to audiences, instead of worrying about what they'll think of me.

Because truthfully, nobody is sitting there going, 'Yeah, she has great lessons that will definitely help me grow my business, but she's clearly not tall enough. I want my money back!' It just doesn't happen. Nobody notices the things we worry about as speakers.

It's so easy to get immersed in ourselves – our content, our wording, our nerves – that we lose focus. Then we focus on the wrong things; we focus on ourselves instead of on our audience.

Remember, your time on stage is about what you *give* to your audience. It's about the lessons you share that your audience members can take away and apply to their own lives to create change.

So, don't get preoccupied with how you'll be perceived. Focus on the most engaging and effective ways to share your message. *What can you teach your audience, and what's the most exciting way that you can share your lessons*?

If you focus on giving your audience the best experience possible, you'll have the best experience in the process.

Everybody wins.

YOU

Now it's your time to inspire

The best speakers **share their gift**. To be in a position where you can help inspire change and motivate others with your ideas is a really special place to be.

We've all lived different lives, and each have our own individual perspectives, insights, and experiences. As a result, we all have valuable lessons to teach each other, and important messages to share.

I know public speaking can feel incredibly nerve-racking, but life is far too short to wonder 'What if…'.

My experiences as a stand-up comedian, author, and public speaker have taught me time and time again that when you follow your heart and take a creative risk, people don't judge you in the way that you imagine. Instead, they respect and support you for having the courage to follow your dreams. And by doing so, you often inspire others to find and follow their dreams too.

So, never underestimate what you're capable of, and the value of sharing your story. You never know who your message will reach and the wonderful ways you can have a positive ripple effect.

And the truth is, in this mad, chaotic, and insane digital era, we all have the power to change the world. Now, more than ever, a single message – **your message** – if it's powerful and delivered in the right way, can reach hundreds and thousands of people in a second.

I hope this pocketbook inspires you to step out of your comfort zone, to fight your fear, to trust your instincts, and to learn to have fun with public speaking. I hope it helps you build the courage and strength needed to share your unique message with the world.

Thank you for investing in yourself by taking the time to read this book. I can't wait to see you shine brightly on stage.

THANK YOU

To the incredible authors and spiritual teachers who have inspired me and changed my life. Your books, live events, meditations, insights, and lessons have helped me grow and transform in incredible ways.

Gabrielle Bernstein
Alan Cohen
Dr Joe Dispenza
Esther and Jerry Hicks (Abraham-Hicks
  Publications)
Anita Moorjani
Oliver Rivers
Tony Robbins
Marianne Williamson

You've opened my mind up to the laws of the Universe, to the magic of creation, to new ways of thinking, to endless possibilities, to the importance of always choosing love over fear, and most of all, you've helped me break through my own limitations.

If it weren't for everything I've learnt from your teachings, I would not have written this book with such effortless joy. In fact, I would probably still be writing it, drafting it, reviewing it, and endlessly second-guessing it.

Instead, I'm just excited to create, share, live, love, teach, inspire, bring joy to others, and above all, trust in a plan greater than my own. And then, when this project is complete, I'm excited to move onto the next awesome creation, and experience the joy *all over again*. Thank you all for your wonderful gifts!

A FEW MORE SPECIAL THANKS

To Mum and Dad, Julie and Joey Borensztajn: Thank you for your unconditional support in every career choice and life decision I've ever made. You've showered me with so much love and strength, and have so much faith and confidence in me, that I'm now in a position where I help others build their confidence levels every day. What a beautiful gift to receive and to be able to give back to the world! I love you.

To Dave Barbour and Angie Summa: If it weren't for you, this pocketbook would have been made up of 48,000 action steps. That sounds more like a suitcase-size book to me which wouldn't fit in anybody's pocket! Thanks for your genius 3-week suggestion and beautiful support through my journey.

To Adam Cubito: Your green ticks are my benchmark for excellence and mean the world to me. Thanks for dreaming up creative ideas to market my book before I even finished writing it. You're a star!

To Shannon Gettins: Thanks for the LOLs, the love, the support, the advice, the edits, the cuts, and the Carls! As always, I couldn't have done this without your amazing help and the endless laughter that we share. You're the best! xxx

To Ashley Tyghe: Thank you for your amazing creative vision and unbelievable video ninja skills. I love your work, your passion, and your creativity. Thanks for the hours you spend splicing and dicing my public speaking videos. You always edit in the perfect shots (except for our bloopers – which I actually love the most!).

To David Longfield: Thank you for making this entire pocketbook process a breeze, from start to finish! It's been so easy and so much fun working on book #2 with you that I'm almost ready to get started on book #3! (Almost...)

ABOUT THE AUTHOR

Jordana Borensztajn is a keynote speaker, presentation skills coach, social media strategist, and humourist.

Jordana was a News Corp Australia journalist, she worked at Nova Entertainment as online music editor, content producer, and social media manager, she speaks at corporate conferences around the world, and she's performed two sold-out shows in the Melbourne International Comedy Festival. Her first book was an educational and entertaining business marketing book called *Capture My Attention: How to Stand Out Online with Creative Content.*

When Jordana's not on stage inspiring audiences with high-energy and interactive keynote presentations and workshops, or helping clients in a one-on-one coaching capacity, she's busy seeking out small animals to take selfies with to boost her Instagram following.

CONNECT WITH JORDANA

Do you want to grow and expand your
public speaking skills further?

Connect with Jordana to discover how her one-on-
one coaching, group workshops, presentations,
and training programs can help you.

jordana@jordanab.com
www.jordanab.com.au
www.communicatewithconfidence.com.au

Connect with Jordana on social media

LinkedIn:	linkedin.com/in/jordanaborensztajn
Instagram:	instagram.com/jordanaborensztajn
Facebook:	facebook.com/iamjordanaborensztajn
Twitter:	twitter.com/JordanaOZ
YouTube:	youtube.com/user/jordanaborensztajn

NEXT STEPS

I have so many helpful public speaking tips, tricks, and techniques that I love sharing with my clients. Choosing my top 21 to feature in this book was next to impossible.

There will *definitely* be a second pocketbook with more steps, more advice and more LOLs, and I would love to include tips that will benefit you.

So, if there is anything you'd like to learn about (in 316 words or less) that I haven't yet covered, email me at **jordana@jordanab.com** and I'll drop it in the suggestion box for pocketbook 2!

Printed in Australia
AUHW010238140222
359550AU00018B/18